J 12

TEXTILES

Meryl Doney

W

FRANKLIN WATTS
A Division of Grolier Publishing
LONDON • NEW YORK • HONG KONG • SYDNEY
DANBURY, CONNECTICUT

CONNOLLY

About this book

In this book we look at the ways in which the making, decorating, and wearing of textiles have developed around the world. We begin with the many exciting techniques for decorating fabric. We then discover how to make fabric by using simple braiding and weaving skills. Finally, we look at some traditional ways in which materials are reused and recycled to make even more beautiful objects.

On the left-hand pages you will find examples of original fabrics, with a map to show where each one comes from. Details of how you can make something using the same techniques of decoration are on the right-hand pages.

Most of the steps are very easy to follow, but where you see this sign ask for help from an adult.

A project to do together

In the isolated rural communities of Europe and North America during the nineteenth century, the art of patchwork and quilting had two important functions. It enabled women to use up scraps of old material to make new fabrics. It was also an important way of keeping in touch with friends and neighbors. At a quilting "bee," everyone would gather at someone's house to work together on a large patchwork quilt. It gave the women a chance to meet and talk and to catch up on local gossip!

On page 29 we suggest a way in which you could renew this old tradition, by getting together with some friends to make a community quilt. The quilt could then be sold to raise funds for a local cause or charity of your choice.

© 1996 Franklin Watts
Text © Meryl Doney 1996

First American Edition 1997 by
Franklin Watts
A Division of Grolier Publishing Co., Inc.
Sherman Turnpike
Danbury, Connecticut 06813

10 9 8 7 6 5 4 3 2 1

Series editor: Kyla Barber
Editor: Jane Walker
Design: Visual Image
Cover design: Kirstie Billingham
Artwork: Ruth Levy
Photography: Peter Millard

Welsh pillow and mirror work embroidery from Maureen Antoniades. Very special thanks to Myra McDonnell, advisor and textile wizard.

Library of Congress Cataloging-in-Publication Data
Doney, Meryl, 1942–
    Textiles/Meryl Doney.
    p.   cm.   — (World crafts)
    Includes bibliographical references and index.
    Summary: Discusses varied types of fabric art from around the world and the techniques used to create them and provides step-by-step instructions for related projects.
        ISBN 0-531-14432-1
        1. Textile crafts —Juvenile literature. 2. Textile fabrics—Juvenile literature. [1. Textile fabrics. 2. Textile crafts. 3. Handicraft.]
    I. Title. II Series: Doney, Meryl, 1942- World Crafts
    TT699.D66 1997
    746—dc20
                                                        96-1308(
                                                        CIP A(

Printed in Great Britain

When Drífa felt the moment of her death approaching, she said to Gríma: "My life is now coming to an end and I am not destined to rest in hallowed ground." She looked up at her friend: "Tomorrow I will go down to the waterfall where I have so often taken pleasure in the beauty of nature. The little waterfalls remind me of the place where I first met Bergsteinn, and there is also a wonderful view from there to Skessuhorn where I said my last farewell to my mother. Now I shall put it to the test, whether my troll's nature works when the morning sun bathes me in its rays. Her expression turned thoughtful and she mused: "The greater part of my life I have spent at Fossatún," and she smiled slightly when the memories of years gone by passed through her mind. Then she went on: "Everything comes to an end except eternity and I want to merge with it here." Gríma looked at her and answered at once: "I shall assume the shape of a troll and stand guard by your side."

Just before dawn, Drífa and Gríma got up and walked slowly down to the river. They stood close together, side by side, and smiled to each other when the first rays of the morning sun appeared in the bright sky. They felt the transformation as their bodies turned stiff and their skin hardened. When the sun had risen fully, their image had been etched into the cliff where they had been standing and looking over the waterfall. Ever since, that spot has been known as Tröllafossar, "Trolls' Falls."

The Last Troll

Tryggðatröll

© Text: Steinar Berg 2007
© Illustration: Brian Pilkington 2007
© Translation: Bernard Scudder
© Photographs: Jóhann Páll Valdimarsson

Fossatún 2013

Designer: Margrét E. Laxness
Printer: Ednas print
Printed in Slovenia

ISBN: 978-9935-9013-2-3

Contents

The world of warp and weft

In prehistoric times, people living in the colder regions of the world needed to protect themselves by making clothes to wear. They used natural materials such as animal skins and fur, woven grass and leaves. Needles were made from bone or thorns, with lengths of grass or animal sinew used as thread. The earliest known fabric is a piece of woven linen, which was found wrapped around a body in an Egyptian tomb. It dates back to around 3000 B.C.

Woven fabrics were produced from plant fibers such as cotton, flax, jute, and hemp. They were also made from animal products such as silk from the cocoon of the silkworm and wool from sheep, goats, camels, llamas, or their cousins, vicuñas. Human hair may also have been used on occasion. Patchwork and embroidery may have developed from the need to darn new patches on old clothes.

Changing the color of fibers by treating them with dyes is also an ancient art. Part of a poncho made from dyed fabric decorated by tying has been found in Peru. It was probably made around 200 B.C. Batik work, which uses a substance such as mud or wax to resist dye and make a design, may have developed in China as long ago as 1000 B.C.

A bewildering variety of textiles and methods of decoration is available to us today. Many of the textiles are manufactured on huge machines, but the principles are still the same as those used to make fabrics by hand. By looking at the beautiful things made in different cultures around the world, we can begin to appreciate the skill and artistry of the people who make and decorate them — and perhaps create new and beautiful things ourselves.

Your own textile-decorating kit

You do not need many expensive pieces of equipment to make and decorate fabrics, but it is useful to have an interesting collection of materials to choose from. You might like to collect a boxful of textiles such as old cotton sheets, velvet, lace, and leather pieces, embroidery, ribbons, and braids. These might be found in your own home, thrift shops, tag or car trunk sales, or from friends and neighbors.

Clean each item before you store it. Always remove buttons, beads, and other decorations from clothes that you are throwing out. Keep them in a box with your sewing equipment.

Here is a list of the most useful items that you will need for making and decorating textiles:

scissors • craft knife • pencil • tape measure • ruler • brushes • fabric paint • masking tape • colored silk and cotton embroidery threads • gold and silver thread • chalk • sewing pins • safety pins • drawing pins • paper • newspaper •

colored inks • felt-tip pens • staple gun and staples • iron and ironing board • needle and thread • sewing machine • rubber gloves • plastic bowl • cold-water dyes • detergent • elastic • tracing paper • wool • polyester stuffing

Some useful stitches

Here are examples of the most common embroidery stitches. You can use several together to build up a design.

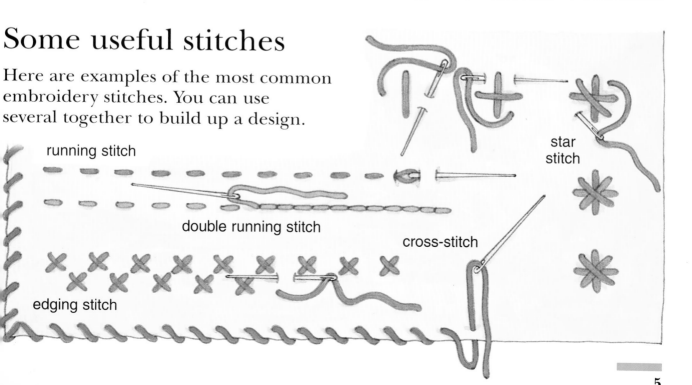

running stitch

double running stitch

star stitch

cross-stitch

edging stitch

Hand-painted banners

Hand painting on cloth is a very ancient art. It probably developed as a kind of portable wall painting. The example shown below is a backdrop for a traveling theater from the northern region of India. The cloth is unrolled and hung up before the play, so that it acts as an advertisement. Once the play begins, the actors use the banner as their backdrop. In a country where many people cannot read, this form of advertising is very useful. Most people will recognize the characters in the picture and will know which play to expect.

In several areas of India these magnificent paintings continue to be made in the traditional way. They are painted carefully, using an outline that prevents the colors from running into each other. The material for the outline is made from a paste, often rice starch, that will wash away once the painting has been colored. It creates a distinctive outlined style of painting.

These hand-painted banners are commonly found in Indian homes too. A *toran* (above), with the traditional flags along the bottom, is strung across the doorway of a house to welcome visitors and to bring good luck.

Make a welcoming *toran*

You could change the message on the flags of your *toran*. It could say "Happy Birthday" or the name of a visitor coming to your home.

You will need: a piece of calico or canvas, 42³/₄ x 10¹/₂ inches (108 x 27 cm) • soft black pencil • ruler • glitter fabric paint • plain fabric paints • brush • scissors • drawing pins

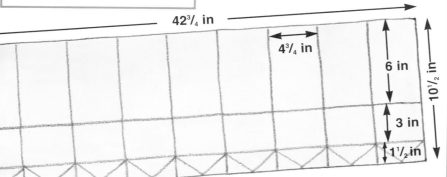

4 Color in the designs with a brush and fabric paints. Leave an extra white edge around each item so that it stands out. Let dry.

1 With pencil, divide up the fabric as shown.

3 Squeeze fabric paint (in squeezable tube) along the outlines of your designs. Let dry.

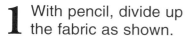

2 Now draw your designs to fit the squares and flag shapes.

5 Cut around the flag shapes and neaten edges. Pin up over your doorway.

CHINA & JAPAN
Painting on silk

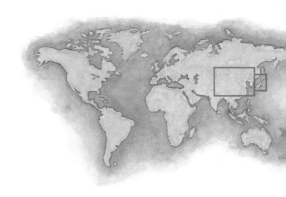

The Far East is famous for the production of silk – a delicate fabric which is woven using thread from the silkworm. The worm winds the fine thread around its cocoon. In ancient times, silk from China and Japan was traded for goods from countries in Europe. In China, a coat made of very fine, transparent silk has been found in a tomb dating back over 1,000 years. Only in recent years, with the help of modern machinery, have we been able to make such fine silk again.

The art of painting on silk developed alongside its weaving. Many famous Chinese and Japanese artists have painted only on silk, and their pictures can be found in museums around the world. This traditional painting (left) has been mounted to form a greeting card, and the modern design (below) has been hand painted onto a scarf.

Make a window panel

The thinner the silk, then the more delicate you can make your painting. If you hold your work up to the light it will shine through the silk, just like a stained-glass window.

Practice painting on a small piece of silk first. The fabric absorbs the paint very easily, and thin brush strokes spread out to become fat ones. Use this method of silk painting to make a scarf like the one shown opposite or the window panel.

You will need: plain silk • scissors • white paper • masking tape • permanent black felt-tip pen • colored inks • brush • jar of water • old saucer (for diluted inks) • iron and ironing board • small picture frame • staple gun and staples or tacks

2 Use the colored inks to paint background colors. Paint dark at the bottom and paler toward the top. Dilute your inks with water for the palest colors.

3 Paint the fish using darker colors on the top and paler colors along the belly, to contrast with the background. Let dry.

4 Iron carefully. Stretch silk across the back of frame. Secure with a staple gun or tacks. Trim edges. Hang up in a window and see the colors glow.

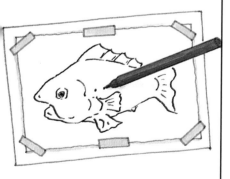

1 Cut a piece of silk a little larger than the frame. Tape the edges to a sheet of white paper. Draw the outline of the fish with the felt-tip pen.

INDIA AND FRANCE

Design by blocks

Block printing was first invented in India as a way of applying dye to fabric. The process used quite complicated mixtures of dyes and chemicals to make a permanent mark on the fabric. The block designs were carved into pieces of hardwood, and great skill was needed to match each print to the next one in order to form the pattern.

Try curling your hand into a fist and then ink the bottom part around your small finger. Now press the inked part onto a piece of paper. Your fist will make a curled pattern similar to the one shown right. This is said to be how the most traditional Indian design (below right) was formed. It is now called "Paisley," after the Scottish town that first copied the shapes from Indian fabric.

Paisley design is still very popular. The finest examples of European block printing, as shown on this head scarf (left), come from France. They are still made by hand, using around 27 different colors printed over each other.

Make a special vest

You can use almost anything to print on fabric: your hand, a shape cut into a potato, or a household object like a thread spool or a sponge. Block printing can also be done on most fabrics, even unusual ones like the velvet used here.

You will need: linoleum tile, 32 x 32 inches (80 x 80 cm) • pencil • cutting tool • 40 inches (1 m) square cotton velvet • scissors • newspaper • brush • fabric paint • iron and ironing board • tape measure • paper • pins • needle • thread

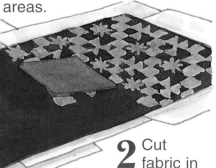

1 Divide linoleum tile into 16 squares as shown. With a pencil, draw this design, or your own design, onto the tile. With cutting tool, remove the background areas.

2 Cut fabric in half. Lay one half flat on newspaper, right side up. Brush paint over the raised parts of the linoleum tile. Press the tile face down onto the fabric and peel off again.

3 Repaint the tile and make the second print next to the first. Repeat until the fabric is covered. Let dry. Fix paint by ironing back of fabric.

4 Take your own measurements for A, B, C, D, E, F, and G. Draw the simple pattern shown here onto paper, using your measurements. Add $^3/_4$ in (2 cm) all around for seams and hems.

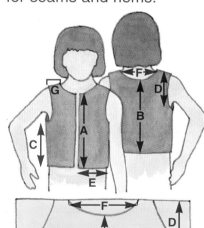

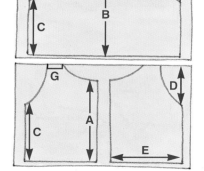

5 Pin pattern onto fabric, using printed fabric for the two front pieces and plain for the back. Cut out fabric. Place right sides together and sew shoulders and sides. Hem all edges.

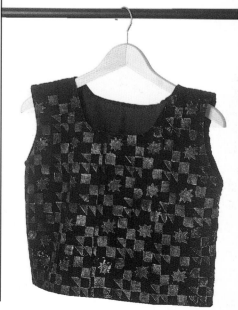

Printing through screens

Screen printing is a relatively modern technique for adding a design to fabric. It was originally developed for printing advertisements and posters on paper. Ink or paint is squeezed through a fine fabric mesh, or screen, onto another surface. Where the holes in the mesh are blocked up, no color will print. The holes can be blocked using anything from a simple paper shape to a photographically produced stencil. Most of the designs on T-shirts are printed in this way.

These shopping bags were printed in Ethiopia (near left) and India (far left) to advertise the shops that supplied them. The T-shirt is a typical example of a garment that has been printed through a photo screen. It was made to advertise a tour by the Irish rock band U2.

Print your own advertising bag

You will need: organza, 14 x 16 inches (35 x 40 cm) • picture frame, 10 x 12 inches (25 x 30 cm) • staple gun and staples • newspaper • felt-tip pen • craft knife • calico or thick cotton, 27 x 15 inches (68 x 38 cm) • scissors • masking tape • spoon • fabric paints • short ruler • rubber gloves • iron and ironing board • sewing machine or needle and thread

1 To make screen, staple a piece of organza (thin silk) or nylon tights across the back of the frame.

2 To make stencils, trace design twice onto two sheets of newspaper.

Using a craft knife, cut out shape to be printed in yellow on first sheet. Cut out shapes to be printed in red on the second sheet.

3 Cut fabric into one large piece and two strips. Fold large piece in half and lay on newspaper.

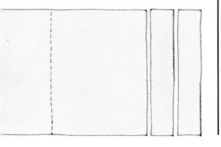

4 Lay first stencil on fabric. Mark position of stencil edges with tape. Place screen over stencil and tape in place.

5 Spoon yellow paint onto screen. Wearing rubber gloves, pull ruler across screen, squeezing paint through screen onto stencil and fabric. Peel screen and stencil from fabric. Wash screen. Let fabric dry.

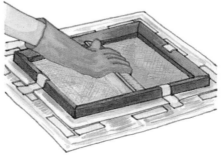

6 Repeat with second stencil, using tape as a guide to position. (Don't forget the middle of the letter O). Let dry.

7 Iron back of fabric to set paint. Turn over top edge of printed fabric and hem. Put right sides together and sew bottom and side seams. For handles, sew fabric strips into tubes. Turn right side out and attach to inside of bag.

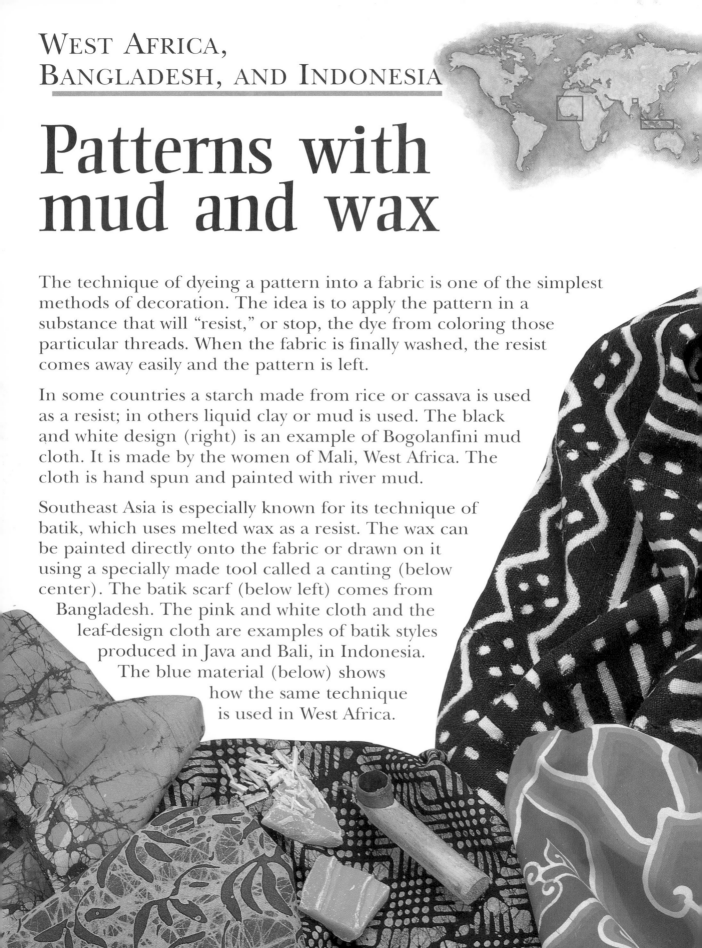

Patterns with mud and wax

The technique of dyeing a pattern into a fabric is one of the simplest methods of decoration. The idea is to apply the pattern in a substance that will "resist," or stop, the dye from coloring those particular threads. When the fabric is finally washed, the resist comes away easily and the pattern is left.

In some countries a starch made from rice or cassava is used as a resist; in others liquid clay or mud is used. The black and white design (right) is an example of Bogolanfini mud cloth. It is made by the women of Mali, West Africa. The cloth is hand spun and painted with river mud.

Southeast Asia is especially known for its technique of batik, which uses melted wax as a resist. The wax can be painted directly onto the fabric or drawn on it using a specially made tool called a canting (below center). The batik scarf (below left) comes from Bangladesh. The pink and white cloth and the leaf-design cloth are examples of batik styles produced in Java and Bali, in Indonesia. The blue material (below) shows how the same technique is used in West Africa.

Make a decorated cloth

We have used an old plastic detergent bottle to dribble the resist onto the fabric, but you could use a cake decorating bag and nozzle instead. Try out your "dribbler" on a spare piece of cotton. Practice controlling the flow and varying the thickness of the paste.

The simple design is based on a square to make it easy to repeat. The deeper the background color, the clearer the resist pattern will be.

You will need: cotton sheeting (from handkerchief size to a whole sheet) • chalk • tape measure • ready-made starch paste (from art supply shop) • empty detergent bottle • cold-water fabric dye (dark color) • plastic bowl • rubber gloves • detergent • iron and ironing board • sewing pins • sewing machine or needle and thread

4 Wash fabric in soapy water until starch is removed. Dry and iron.

5 Fold in the edges all the way around the fabric and secure with pins. Hem edges and remove pins.

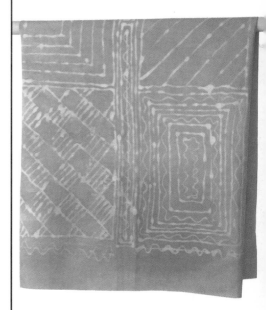

2 Fill bottle dribbler with starch paste. Outline each square and add a pattern. Let dry.

3 Mix dye in a plastic bowl according to the instructions. (Wear rubber gloves when handling dye.) Put fabric with starch patterns into the bowl of dye and leave for 20 minutes. Take out and let dry again.

1 Lay fabric flat on a large working surface. Measure out a grid of lines across the fabric and mark with chalk.

INDIA, WEST AFRICA, AND JAPAN

Tie-dye patterns

Another method of creating a pattern on cloth is to use threads or knots to prevent the dye from reaching parts of the material. This process is known as tie-dyeing.

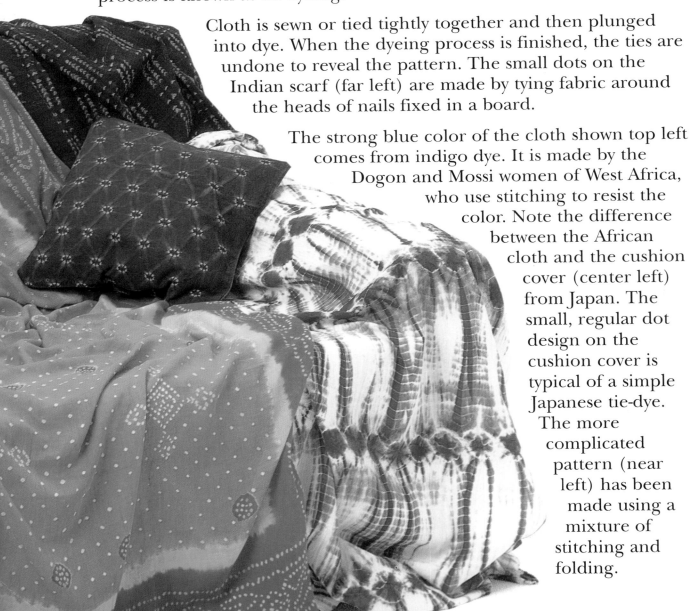

Cloth is sewn or tied tightly together and then plunged into dye. When the dyeing process is finished, the ties are undone to reveal the pattern. The small dots on the Indian scarf (far left) are made by tying fabric around the heads of nails fixed in a board.

The strong blue color of the cloth shown top left comes from indigo dye. It is made by the Dogon and Mossi women of West Africa, who use stitching to resist the color. Note the difference between the African cloth and the cushion cover (center left) from Japan. The small, regular dot design on the cushion cover is typical of a simple Japanese tie-dye. The more complicated pattern (near left) has been made using a mixture of stitching and folding.

Make a colorful scrunchie

You will need: silk or fine cotton, 18½ x 6½ inches (47 x 17 cm) • beads • cotton thread • cold-water fabric dye • plastic bowl • rubber gloves • scissors • iron and ironing board • elastic, 5 inches (12 cm) long • needle

Tie-dyeing can be used to decorate many kinds of material. Silk is particularly good because it is fine and absorbs dye well. When you have decorated your piece of silk, use it to make a scarf, a handkerchief, a wall hanging, or the hair scrunchie shown here.

1 Lay a bead on the fabric. Gather the fabric around it, forming a shape like a head and neck. Wind thread tightly around "neck" and tie. Repeat at intervals until the whole fabric is tied up.

2 Wearing rubber gloves, make up cold-water dye in a plastic bowl. Put your fabric into the dye and leave for 20 minutes.

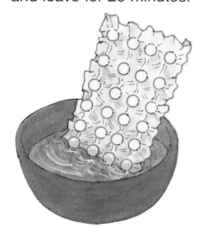

3 Take out the fabric and rinse. Let dry with the beads in place.

4 Cut thread and remove beads. Iron the fabric.

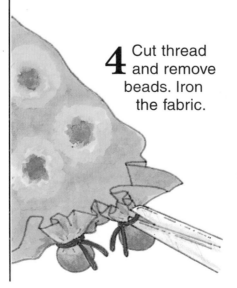

5 Place right sides of fabric together and sew into a tube. Turn the right side out and thread with elastic. Knot elastic in a circle. Sew the ends of the tube together to form a circular hair scrunchie.

Decorating with appliqué work

A completely different way of decorating fabric is to add color and texture by sewing or attaching decoration to its surface. The word "appliqué" means applied, and it describes a method of stitching patches onto fabric. At first this was a way of mending holes in worn clothes, but it soon developed into a method of creating complex and beautiful decorations.

Every culture has its own fabric styles and favorite patterns of appliqué. In cold mountainous regions, felted wool is used for warmth. It is made into coats, rugs and even tents. The felt is often decorated with embroidery and appliqué like this bag from Poland.

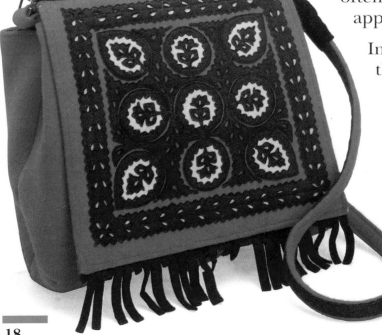

In many South American countries the art of appliqué has been extended to include wall hangings. The one from Chile (above) shows scenes of local life. The picture is made by sewing patches of different-colored fabrics to the surface, using cross stitch. Small doll figures made from fabric and wool have been added to the picture.

Make a felt purse

You will need: one piece of dark-colored (blue) and one piece of light-colored (red) felt, 12 x 6 inches (30 x 15 cm) each • pencil • tracing paper • scissors • sewing pins • thick cotton embroidery thread • needle and thread

This little purse is made from felt and is decorated with a dog motif that comes from Russia. You could use the appliqué dog motif to decorate a jumper or a birthday gift. You may also like to make a Chilean-style appliqué panel that represents scenes from your neighborhood, family, or school.

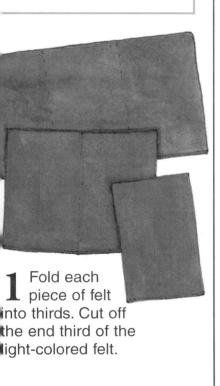

1 Fold each piece of felt into thirds. Cut off the end third of the light-colored felt.

2 Trace the dog pattern onto the small piece of felt. Cut out.

3 Fold dark-colored felt into thirds and place dog motif on front flap. Sew dog pattern onto felt by following the outline with a running stitch (see page 5).

4 Place the light-colored felt on the back of the appliquéd piece. Pin and tack in position.

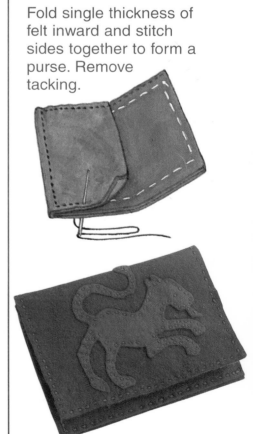

Fold single thickness of felt inward and stitch sides together to form a purse. Remove tacking.

Stitches and mirrors

Embroidery is the art of decorating fabrics using stitching made with colored threads. Wonderfully detailed pictures and designs can be achieved, but it is slow and painstaking work. In the past, it was considered a fitting occupation for suitable "gentlewomen and young ladies." The sampler (right) was made in 1795 by the young Eliza Hall to demonstrate her skill. It is now at the Fitzwilliam Museum in Cambridge, England.

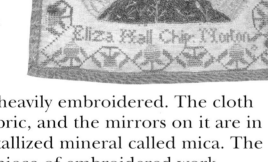

The spectacular embroidery of Gujerat in northern India uses many different stitches, appliqué, and small mirrors. Very small pieces of shiny metal are sewn onto the fabric, which is then heavily embroidered. The cloth shown left is a very old piece of fabric, and the mirrors on it are in fact made from a thin, shiny crystallized mineral called mica. The hat has been made from an old piece of embroidered work.

In more modern times, small mirrors are used, and other additions like shells and buttons can be added. The bag below right is a typical example. The stitching used to attach the mirrors is very small, and every edge is covered in thread so that each piece of mirror is held firmly in place.

Make an embroidered hat

The mirrors on this hat are made with mirror foil — a thin plastic that can be stitched quite easily.

You will need: tape measure • pencil • stiff fabric such as linen, $23\frac{1}{2}$ x $15\frac{1}{2}$ inches (60 x 40 cm) • scissors • iron and ironing board • sewing machine or needle and thread • mirror foil • colored embroidery thread • buttons • beads

1 Measure your head from front to back and side to side at A and B. Mark measurements on the fabric. Cut out an oval shape.

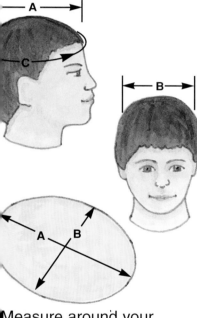

Measure around your forehead at C. Cut a band of fabric $3\frac{1}{2}$ inches (9 cm) wide and as long as your C measurement. Fold in half and iron flat.

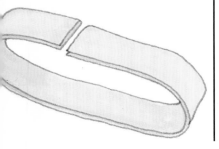

2 Make up the hat by sewing the top piece to the band on the inside. Sew the ends of the band together.

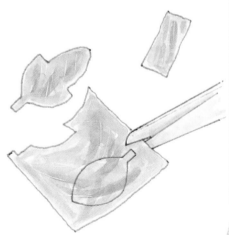

3 Cut different shapes out of the mirror foil.

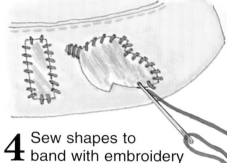

4 Sew shapes to band with embroidery thread using edging stitch (see page 5).

5 Sew buttons and beads between mirror patches. Use the stitches shown on page 5 to add extra patterns.

AFGHANISTAN

Plaited braid

We have been looking at ways to decorate fabrics, but how are fabrics made in the first place? The plaited braid is one of the earliest methods of making fabric, and examples have been found in tombs dating from the Iron Age, which began between 1500 and 1000 B.C.

The nomadic peoples of desert areas are always on the move with their animals. Therefore, they need a method of making fabrics that uses very simple equipment. Plaiting requires only your fingers and no other equipment, so it is an ideal method. The braids or bands are generally made by the men and are used as camel straps to tie down bundles for traveling. They are also used as belts. This decorative camel harness (left) comes from Afghanistan. It has been braided and decorated with shells and tassels.

The braiding method is still used today. This nylon towing rope (right) is braided in exactly the same way as the camel strap, and is very strong.

Braid your own belt

Braiding may seem quite hard to do, but once you have mastered the technique it is very easy. You will see that the braid grows quickly. You can add more colors to change the pattern. You could make a tie, a friendship bracelet, or a purse as well as this belt.

You will need: 24 lengths of wool, 12 blue and 12 yellow — 60-inch (150-cm) lengths make a 30-inch (75-cm) belt • length of string • scissors • needle • thread • belt buckle

1 Bunch all the wool strands together and tie a knot in one end. Use string to tie knot to back of chair. Part the strands in half, with 6 blue strands and 6 yellow strands on each side. Work flat on a table.

2 Hold right half of bunch in right hand. With tip of your forefinger go across to left half and pull up alternate threads.

3 When you reach the end of the bunch, grab the last thread and pull it back through the wool to the middle. Add it to the strands in your right hand.

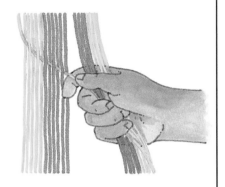

4 Now hold left-hand bunch in left hand. With left forefinger, pick up every alternate thread in right bunch. Take the last thread through the tunnel of threads back to the middle, and add it to the strands in your left hand.

5 Repeat, keeping the work flat as you go, until the braid is as long as you need. To finish both ends of the braid, knot each thread to its neighbor to stop the braid from unwinding.

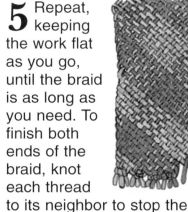

6 Cut off excess wool. Turn one end over and sew down. Sew buckle to other end as shown.

PERU, FINLAND, GHANA, AND AFGHANISTAN

Threads and looms

Weaving is a method of joining together two sets of threads by interlacing them at right angles to one another. The set of threads that travels in parallel lines away from the weaver is called the warp. The set of horizontal threads is the weft. Weaving can be done on a very simple kind of loom called a strap loom. The warp is tied to an object and pulled tight, using a strap that is tied around the weaver's waist. This Peruvian woman (left) is using a strap loom to weave cloth.

This type of weaving produces only strips of cloth that can be sewn together to make any size of fabric. The colorful strips below right are examples of the braid still woven in Finland. Each family has its own distinctive design, which is used to identify their belongings. The long strip (left) is an example of *kente* cloth, which is woven by the Ashanti people of Ghana.

One of the finest examples of weaving and tie-dyeing being used together is in a fabric called ikat. The warp threads are accurately dyed before weaving. The example below is from Afghanistan.

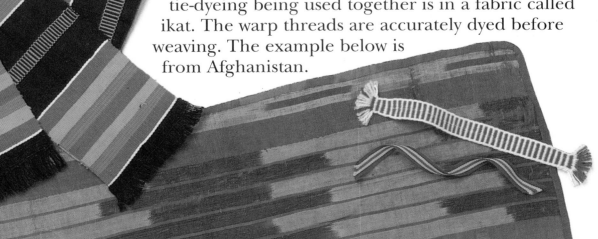

Weave on your own loom

You will need: tape measure • wool • string • ¹/₂-inch (1-cm) dowel, 20 inches (50 cm) long • masking tape • knitting safety pin • knitting needle • scissors • darning needle • thread

1 Measure from your chest to your toes. Make a 12-strand skein of wool the same length. Tie a knot in one end and put loop over your big toe.

2 Run the string around your back and tie one end to the dowel. Tape in place. Pass end of wool skein over dowel. Tie free end of string to the other end of the dowel. Arrange wool loops evenly along the dowel.

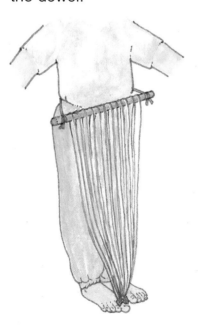

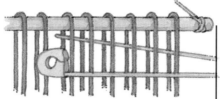

3 Thread open safety pin from left to right, picking up alternate warp threads. Close pin.

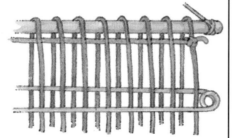

4 Tie end of weft wool to left-hand warp. Lift safety pin and run weft through gap between warp threads. Pull pin toward you to straighten weft.

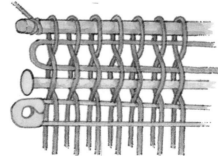

5 Move safety pin away from you. Thread a knitting needle from right to left, picking up different alternate threads. Lift needle and repeat weaving as before. Do not pull ends of rows too tight.

6 Repeat weaving process (removing and reweaving the knitting needle each time) until weaving reaches the length desired.

7 To finish, pull out dowel and cut warp loops. Using a darning needle, sew each thread at one end back into the woven strip. Leave a long fringe at the other end and knot threads in groups of four.

WALES AND INDIA

The art of quilting

Quilting was an early way of making clothes and coverings warmer for the winter. In China, beautiful quilted silk coats were made to keep out the cold. They consisted of three layers: a plain backing sheet, a layer of padding, and a silk top sheet. These layers were sewn together with tiny running stitches to outline a pattern, a picture, or to form a grid of diamonds or squares.

In Great Britain, a form of plain white quilting using white thread became popular. It is known as "Welsh quilting" because the people of Wales have developed it into a national art. This silk cushion shows how the stitching forms the pattern.

A quilt style known as trapunto, or stuffed work, was developed in Italy. It consists of two layers of fabric that are sewn together with running stitches. Small amounts of stuffing are then inserted through the backing fabric, to make the patterns stand out. The elephant on the Indian bag shown top right is quilted in this way.

Make a quilted brooch

This decorated panel is made out of a shiny gold fabric using a combination of Welsh and trapunto quilting. It could be used to decorate a coat or the top of a box. The panel shown here makes an unusual brooch, or pin.

You will need: two small pieces of gold lamé fabric • polyester stuffing • pins • soft black pencil • gold thread • needle • scissors • small gold bead • brooch pin or safety pin

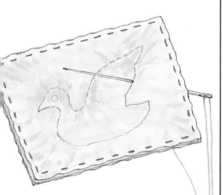

1 Sandwich the stuffing between the two pieces of gold fabric. Pin down the edges and tack.

2 Draw your design on the fabric with pencil. Sew the outline of the swan (or any animal) using small stitches. Use a double thickness of gold thread.

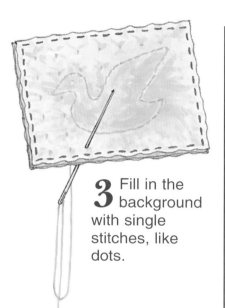

3 Fill in the background with single stitches, like dots.

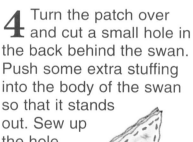

4 Turn the patch over and cut a small hole in the back behind the swan. Push some extra stuffing into the body of the swan so that it stands out. Sew up the hole.

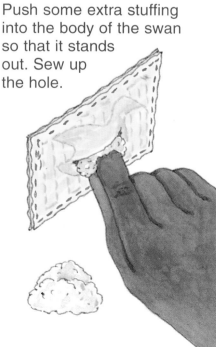

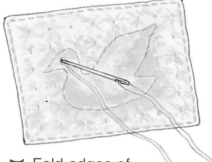

5 Fold edges of fabric to the back and secure with running stitches. Sew on a gold bead for the eye. Attach a brooch pin to the back of your panel.

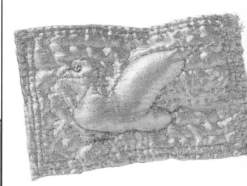

Patchwork everybody

In seventeenth-century England, patchwork quilts became popular as a way of using up pieces of the wonderful fabrics imported from the East Indies. When the early settlers traveled to North America, they took their patchwork craft with them.

The tradition has continued until today, and American patchwork, or "pieced work," quilts (see left) have become famous throughout the world. Many traditional patterns have names like "log cabin," "star of hope," and "Jacob's ladder."

Families often lived on isolated farms or in small religious communities such as the Mennonites and the Amish people. The women used to meet together for quilting "bees." Everyone would sew the patchwork pieces together and then gather around a quilting frame to make the running stitches all over the quilt's surface. While they worked, the women used to tell stories, swap recipes, and catch up on the local news.

Make a community quilt

A community quilt is a fun way to involve your friends and family in making something together. Hopefully, the finished product will be a beautiful object that you can either give to someone special or sell to raise money.

Cut several large pieces of plain-colored fabric into 6-inch squares and give one to each person. Ask them to decorate the fabric — by embroidering or writing their name, sewing a picture on it, or making a handprint. Or ask people to supply squares of material from their favorite old clothes.

You will need: fabric patches prepared by friends (60 squares make a cot-size quilt) • pins • sewing machine • needle • thread • iron and ironing board • an old blanket or length of padding • a backing sheet • length of 1½-inch (4-cm) ribbon

2 Pin the first two squares, right sides together. Sew a ½-inch (1-cm) hem along one side. Press open. Repeat with the next squares to form strips. Pin and sew all the strips together.

4 Sew a ribbon around the edges to finish off the quilt.

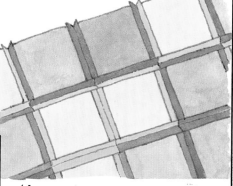

(Accurate measurement is important to make sure that the squares lie flat.) Iron squares flat.

1 Lay out your squares so that they form an interesting pattern.

3 Make a sandwich of the completed patchwork, padding, and backing sheet. Sew along the strips through all three layers.

Useful information

Museums

American Craft Museum
40 West 53rd Street
New York, NY 10019
Tel: 212-956-3535
Fax: 212-956-3699
(American 20th-century crafts by artists working in glass; textiles; wood; ceramic and metal media)

Cooper-Hewitt National
Museum of Design
Smithsonian Institution
2 East 91st Street
New York, NY 10128
Tel: 212-860-6868
Fax: 212-860-6909
(design and decorative arts of all periods and countries; architecture and design drawings; textiles; wallpaper; prints; graphics; woodwork; metalwork; ceramics; glass; furniture)

Museum of American Folk Art
61 West 62nd Street
New York, NY 10023
Tel: 212-977-7170
Fax: 212-977-8134
(American 18th- to 20th-century folk sculpture and painting; textile arts; decorative arts; environmental folk art; history)

Organizations

American Home Sewing and
Craft Association
1375 Broadway
New York, NY 10018
Tel: 212-302-2150
Fax: 212-391-8009

American Quilter's Society
P.O. Box 3290
Paducah, KY 42001
Tel: 502-898-7903
Fax: 502-898-8890

Handweavers Guild of
America
2402 University Avenue W,
Suite 702
St. Paul, MN 55114
Tel: 612-646-0802
Fax: 612-646-0806

National Quilting Association
P.O. Box 393
Ellicott, MD 21041
Tel: 410-461-5733
Fax: 410-313-2790

Books

African Crafts
by Judith Hoffman Corwin
(Watts, 1990)

African Crafts
by Jane Kerina
(Lion Books, 1970)

Arts and Crafts from Around the House
by Imogene Forte
(Incentive Publications, 1983)

Asian Crafts
by Judith Hoffman Corwin
(Watts, 1992)

Batik and Tie-Dye
by Susie O'Reilly
(Thomson Learning, 1993)

Fabric Art
by John Lancaster
(Watts, 1991)

Fun with Fabrics
by Juliet Bawden
(Random Books for Young Readers, 1993)

My Grandmother's Patchwork Quilt
by Jane Bolton
(Doubleday, 1994)

Textiles
by Susie O'Reilly
(Watts, 1991)

Things I Can Make with Cloth
by Sabine Lohf
(Chronicle, 1989)

Using Yarn, Fabric & Thread
(Marshall Cavendish, 1991)

Weaving
by Susie O'Reilly
(Thomson Learning, 1993)

Glossary

Amish A strict religious group found mostly in North America. The Amish separated from a group of Christians called the Mennonites (see below).

appliqué A kind of decoration made by sewing one material on top of another.

braiding Weaving threads across each other to form a piece of material.

batik A technique of decorating fabric by using melted wax to stop dye from reaching some parts of the fabric.

community A group of people who live in one place.

felt Cloth that is made by pressing together wool or other fibers.

fiber A thin strand or thread that makes up a material or fabric.

grid A pattern of lines that are drawn at right angles to each other.

hemp A woody plant with strong fibers. The fibers are used to make rope.

ikat A fabric design that is made by dyeing threads before weaving them.

indigo A blue dye made from a plant.

jute Fiber from the jute plant. It is used to make items such as sacking and mats.

loom A machine for weaving cloth.

Mennonites A Christian religious group whose members have a simple lifestyle and way of worship.

mica A mineral found in the rock granite.

nomadic Describes the lifestyle of traveling people who move around, usually in desert areas, to find pasture and water for their animals.

poncho A short, cloak-like coat worn in Central and South America.

resist In fabric decoration, a substance that stops dye from reaching the fibers.

tie-dye To decorate fabric using threads or knots to stop dye from reaching some parts of the fabric.

transparent See-through.

warp The vertical threads in a piece of weaving.

weaving Joining together two sets of threads, at right angles to each other, to make a piece of cloth.

weft The horizontal threads in a piece of weaving.

Index

Additional photographs:

page 20, Fitzwilliam Museum, University of Cambridge/Bridgeman Art Library, London; page 24 (top), Christopher Rennie/Robert Harding Picture Library, London.